The
Labyrinth
Guided
Journal

ISBN: 978-0-9882731-2-2

The Labyrinth Guided Journal

A Year in the Labyrinth

Walk your own journey
as you explore how labyrinths expand
relaxation, respite, healing, spiritual connection,
meditation, prayer, wisdom, intuition,
purpose, grounding, and peace.

Aliyah Schick

Sacred Imprints

The Labyrinth

The twists and turns of the labyrinth remove you from ordinary life, and draw you deeper into willingness, into yourself, and into sacred wisdom. As you walk you enter a meditative, prayerful state that opens you to higher understanding, purpose, answers, and healing.

Walk a labyrinth for relaxation, for respite, for healing, for spiritual connection, for answers, for exploring who you are, for meditation, for prayer, for going deeper, for peace.

Walk once, walk regularly, walk every day.

Walk on foot, or with your finger or a pointer, or with your eyes or your imagination.

Walking a labyrinth can expand intuition, wisdom, and possibilities, ignite personal growth, and enliven your consciousness.

Walking a labyrinth brings you into balance and calm, and allows you to access the best of yourself and to learn to be more of who you are meant to be.

The Labyrinth Guided Journal

Use The Labyrinth Guided Journal to explore your own journey through the next year.

Each week the journal offers a new thought or experience or challenge drawn from the labyrinth, and a question or suggestion for you to consider and write about throughout the week.

A labyrinth is said to be a microcosm of life, focusing your steps, taking you deeper into clarity, understanding, and spiritual connection. Immerse yourself in the expansive benefits and richness of the labyrinth experiece as you write in this journal every day.

The
Weeks

Week One

A labyrinth walk can be many things. Sometimes I walk to release stress or anxiety, or to refocus, or to find solid ground. Sometimes I'm looking for guidance. Sometimes it's to take a mini-vacation. Sometimes I simply have no reason and wonder if one will show up.

This week: What would you like from a labyrinth walk today? "Walk" the labyrinth on the back of this book with your finger or a pointer, and write about what you discover.

Sunday ....

....

....

....

....

....

....

Monday ....

....

....

....

....

....

....

Tuesday ....

....

....

....

....

....

....

Wednesday ....
....
....
....
....
....
....

Thursday ....
....
....
....
....
....
....

Friday ....
....
....
....
....
....
....

Saturday ....
....
....
....
....
....
....

Week Two

I try to keep track of where I am in the labyrinth. It might work at first, but the loops and direction changes disorient me until I give up and just walk. It becomes about the journey, not about the goal. And then coming upon the center is a wonderful surprise.

This week: Let go of a goal today, and instead pay attention to the journey. There is a lot to be noticed and learned and appreciated along the way. Write about what comes up.

Sunday ....

....

....

....

....

....

....

Monday ....

....

....

....

....

....

....

Tuesday ....

....

....

....

....

....

....

Wednesday ....
....
....
....
....
....
....

Thursday ....
....
....
....
....
....
....

Friday ....
....
....
....
....
....

Saturday ....
....
....
....
....
....
....

Week Three

What is the etiquette in a labyrinth when we come face-to-face with a stranger on the same path? Do we both have to step one foot off our path and onto the next path? I really don't like stepping off the path. It feels wrong, like it breaks the pattern or the process. I want to stay on the path, unwaveringly, until the end.

This week: Watch for times when you give way, or don't. How does it feel? How does it feel when you do the opposite?

Sunday

Monday

Tuesday

Wednesday

....
....
....
....
....
....
....

Thursday

....
....
....
....
....
....
....

Friday

....
....
....
....
....
....

Saturday

....
....
....
....
....
....
....

Week Four

Coming to the turn at the end of a medium length run about halfway into the labyrinth, I just can't do another turn right now. I've come so far, done so many turns, been so patient and diligent, and really, really, really want to be done instead of caught in this sense of having climbed ever deeper into complexity. So I stop and just stand there, breathing, for what must be ten whole minutes. Until it finally feels okay to continue.

This week: Today watch for an impulse to stop and breathe. Do you listen to it or go on as usual? What happens?

Sunday ....
....
....
....
....
....
....

Monday ....
....
....
....
....
....
....

Tuesday ....
....
....
....
....
....
....

Wednesday ....

....

....

....

....

....

....

Thursday ....

....

....

....

....

....

....

Friday ....

....

....

....

....

....

Saturday ....

....

....

....

....

....

....

Week Five

Wouldn't it be great if we could close our eyes as we walk the labyrinth? Then we could really focus, no distractions, and go even deeper. But we have to watch where we're going, purposefully place our steps, and be able to adjust to what we encounter.

This week: Are there situations in your life where you need to pay more attention, keep your eyes open, watch where you're going, and make more conscious choices?

Sunday ....

....

....

....

....

....

....

Monday ....

....

....

....

....

....

....

Tuesday ....

....

....

....

....

....

....

Wednesday

Thursday

Friday

Saturday

Week Six

I sit on the ground in the center of the labyrinth and open my heart. Like French doors swung wide open in sunshine and warmth. No need to design what happens next, or even know. A great, two-way flow at once both empties and fills me. I feel part of life, connected, belonging. This must be the absolute best I can ever possibly feel.

This week: Open your heart at least once each day, in a labyrinth or elsewhere. What happens?

Sunday ....
....
....
....
....
....
....

Monday ....
....
....
....
....
....
....

Tuesday ....
....
....
....
....
....
....

Wednesday ....
....
....
....
....
....
....

Thursday ....
....
....
....
....
....

Friday ....
....
....
....
....
....

Saturday ....
....
....
....
....
....
....

Week Seven

A labyrinth is a life-size sacred geometry form, both physical and spiritual at the same time. Its geometric structure creates a very grounded, and grounding, physical experience as we plant each foot on the path, moving our bodies through its patterns. And at the same time the labyrinth is a spiritual, mystical space where we access our higher knowing, guidance, and sacred connections. We, ourselves, are this same paradox of being both physical and spirit at the same time.

This week: How do you benefit from being both physical and spiritual?

Sunday ....
....
....
....
....
....
....

Monday ....
....
....
....
....
....
....

Tuesday ....
....
....
....
....
....
....

Wednesday

Thursday

Friday

Saturday

Week Eight

Oh good, this labyrinth is a small one. It'll go fast and I can get on with the rest of my day. Let's get this over with.

This week: Are you rushing through a potentially valuable practice with minimal effort and attention? Doing it only so you can check it off and say you did it? What would it take to slow down and allow that experience to go deeper? This week refocus that practice and see how that feels.

Sunday ....

....

....

....

....

....

....

Monday ....

....

....

....

....

....

....

Tuesday ....

....

....

....

....

....

....

Wednesday ---

Thursday --

Friday ---

Saturday --

Week Nine

Which labyrinth design shall I build? The ancient, organic style from prehistoric petroglyphs? Or a more geometric, medieval European labyrinth? Or maybe an innovative, creative, artsy design? We make choices all day long, some trivial, some permanent. A labyrinth's construction is not easily changed. How do I choose a design I'll like for years to come?

This week: What choices are you making throughout this day? How do you choose?

Sunday _____
_____
_____
_____
_____
_____
_____

Monday _____
_____
_____
_____
_____
_____
_____

Tuesday _____
_____
_____
_____
_____
_____
_____

Wednesday

Thursday

Friday

Saturday

Week Ten

I'm not even sure why I'm walking this labyrinth today. There's no question to answer, no problem on my mind, no request seeking fulfullment. I'm just here, breathing in and out through this time outside of the everyday, moving through its guided steps in an ancient sacred pattern, into the center and back out again, without ever grasping why.

This week: Do something without knowing why you're doing it. Watch for what may result, and write about it.

Sunday ....
....
....
....
....
....
....

Monday ....
....
....
....
....
....
....

Tuesday ....
....
....
....
....
....
....

Wednesday

_____

_____

_____

_____

_____

_____

_____

Thursday

_____

_____

_____

_____

_____

_____

Friday

_____

_____

_____

_____

_____

_____

Saturday

_____

_____

_____

_____

_____

_____

_____

Week 11

Walking in a familiar local park, to my surprise I stumble upon a labyrinth I've never seen before. Was this here all along and I always passed by without noticing it? Or, did a whole crew of people build it yesterday? Or, did it spring up overnight like a crop circle? I enter into the mystery, become part of it, and walk the labyrinth.

This week: Watch for surprises, and take the time to enjoy them.

Sunday

....

....

....

....

....

....

....

Monday

....

....

....

....

....

....

....

Tuesday

....

....

....

....

....

....

....

Wednesday _____

_____

_____

_____

_____

_____

_____

Thursday _____

_____

_____

_____

_____

_____

Friday _____

_____

_____

_____

_____

_____

Saturday _____

_____

_____

_____

_____

_____

_____

Week 12

Sometimes an answer pops up as soon as I step into the center of a labyrinth. Sometimes it takes a while. Sometimes no answer comes. Sometimes I simply sit and meditate. I rarely turn right around and head back out, just in case something precious might happen there.

This week: What happens to you when you step into the center of a labyrinth? What happens to you when you step into this labyrinth guided journal writing each day?

Sunday ....
....
....
....
....
....
....

Monday ....
....
....
....
....
....
....

Tuesday ....
....
....
....
....
....
....

Wednesday ....

Thursday ....

Friday ....

Saturday ....

Week 13

It's a long way back out from a labyrinth's center. Do we need all that? Couldn't a path half as long serve just fine? Or are there benefits to taking just as long to re-enter life as it took to delve into our inner core?

This week: Explore slower transitions from one activity to another. Are there benefits?

Sunday

_____

_____

_____

_____

_____

_____

_____

Monday

_____

_____

_____

_____

_____

_____

_____

Tuesday

_____

_____

_____

_____

_____

_____

_____

Wednesday ....
....
....
....
....
....
....

Thursday ....
....
....
....
....
....
....

Friday ....
....
....
....
....
....

Saturday ....
....
....
....
....
....
....

Week 14

I saw a stranger stretched out flat on the ground in the center of the labyrinth. After we each finished and headed for our cars I asked her what she had been doing. "Loving on Mother Earth," she said with a big grin. "Does it help to lie on the ground?" I asked. "Oh, yes," she said, "then every bit of me is hugging her, and she is hugging me back. Try it. You'll like it."

This week: What are you doing this week to love on Mother Earth and be loved by her?

Sunday ....
....
....
....
....
....
....

Monday ....
....
....
....
....
....
....

Tuesday ....
....
....
....
....
....
....

Wednesday ....

Thursday ....

Friday ....

Saturday ....

Week 15

Walking a labyrinth is meditative, but it's very different from a seated meditation. It's more like being out in life, engaged with its influences, responding to its happenings. In order to experience the labyrinth's journey you go where its pathways and turnings lead, and cooperate with its patterns.

This week: Watch for how you cooperate with life's twists and turns each day. Does life lead you to something meaningful, to a realization or message or expansion of some kind?

Sunday _____

_____

_____

_____

_____

_____

_____

Monday _____

_____

_____

_____

_____

_____

_____

Tuesday _____

_____

_____

_____

_____

_____

_____

Wednesday ....

....

....

....

....

....

....

Thursday ....

....

....

....

....

....

....

Friday ....

....

....

....

....

....

Saturday ....

....

....

....

....

....

....

Week 16

Some labyrinths are small and simple, with only a few quick turns. Others are large and complex, sending us this way and that, inward and outward, looping back and forth till we wonder will we ever get to the center. But every labyrinth has its center. If we are patient, committed, and carry on, we get to the center, every time.

This week: Each day watch for times you stay with one task until you get to where you want to be. How does it feel?

Sunday ....
....
....
....
....
....
....

Monday ....
....
....
....
....
....
....

Tuesday ....
....
....
....
....
....
....

Wednesday --

Thursday ---

Friday ---

Saturday ---

Week 17

Today I would really like to be alone in the labyrinth. No one following behind or catching up to me and passing. No one ahead so I adjust my progress to theirs. No one coming at me head on, so one of us has to step off the path. No one catching my eye, or speaking to me, or surprising me. No one else's pace or process or pattern. Just me, alone in the labyrinth.

This week: What would you like to do alone today?

Sunday ....
....
....
....
....
....
....

Monday ....
....
....
....
....
....
....

Tuesday ....
....
....
....
....
....
....

Wednesday _____

_____

_____

_____

_____

_____

_____

Thursday _____

_____

_____

_____

_____

_____

Friday _____

_____

_____

_____

_____

_____

Saturday _____

_____

_____

_____

_____

_____

_____

Week 18

There's a large basket at the entrance to this labyrinth, and a sign inviting us to leave all our concerns and chores and burdens here. It says we can pick them up again when we leave. If we want to.

This week: Today when you walk the dog, or go to the gym, or watch a movie, when you soak in a tub, take a work break, eat a meal, drive in your car, or another situation with a beginning and end, leave your worries in a basket as you begin. Pick them up again at the end, if you want to.

Sunday ....
....
....
....
....
....
....

Monday ....
....
....
....
....
....
....

Tuesday ....
....
....
....
....
....
....

Wednesday _____

_____

_____

_____

_____

_____

_____

Thursday _____

_____

_____

_____

_____

_____

_____

Friday _____

_____

_____

_____

_____

_____

Saturday _____

_____

_____

_____

_____

_____

_____

Week 19

A labyrinth doesn't let us charge right at our goal. It insists that we meander, and at times it even sends us directly opposite from our goal. We circle all the way around the center and back again, covering every possible path on our way there. We only step into the center after every other option has been explored. When there is nowhere else to go except in.

This week: What choice or decision are you heading for where that kind of thorough preparation would be good? This week dig deeper into it.

Sunday _____

_____

_____

_____

_____

_____

_____

Monday _____

_____

_____

_____

_____

_____

_____

Tuesday _____

_____

_____

_____

_____

_____

_____

Wednesday ....
....
....
....
....
....
....

Thursday ....
....
....
....
....
....
....

Friday ....
....
....
....
....
....
....

Saturday ....
....
....
....
....
....
....

Week 20

I'm taking the Labyrinths Meditative Coloring Book and a set of fine-tip markers with me on my trip. I'll be able to color my way through a labyrinth wherever I am, in waiting rooms, on airplanes, in the hotel at the end of the day, and at the Grand Canyon. (www.MeditativeColoring.com/labyrinths)

This week: Where would you like to be able to bring your own labyrinth to walk? There are ways. Explore your options for portable labyrinths.

Sunday ....
....
....
....
....
....
....

Monday ....
....
....
....
....
....
....

Tuesday ....
....
....
....
....
....
....

Wednesday ....

....

....

....

....

....

....

Thursday ....

....

....

....

....

....

....

Friday ....

....

....

....

....

....

....

Saturday ....

....

....

....

....

....

....

Week 21

I stopped in the labyrinth to watch geese fly overhead, and got turned around. I think I might be going in the wrong direction now. It's hard to tell in a labyrinth. All I can do is carry on and end up either at the center or back at the beginning.

This week: Are you heading for where you want to be? If not, what can you do today to turn yourself around to what feels right?

Sunday

Monday

Tuesday

Wednesday _____
_____
_____
_____
_____
_____
_____

Thursday _____
_____
_____
_____
_____
_____
_____

Friday _____
_____
_____
_____
_____
_____
_____

Saturday _____
_____
_____
_____
_____
_____
_____

Week 22

Shall I build a labyrinth in my far-from-level backyard? Walking its path will take me up and down as well as in and out. I could labor at smoothing it out some, but perhaps its odd bobbles and bumps would be a more authentic representation of life than a flat, smooth, perfect labyrinth.

This week: What in your life adds an extra dimension of complication beyond the ordinary twists and turns? How do you respond? Write about what works well.

Sunday
....
....
....
....
....
....
....

Monday
....
....
....
....
....
....
....

Tuesday
....
....
....
....
....
....
....

Wednesday ....
....
....
....
....
....
....

Thursday ....
....
....
....
....
....
....

Friday ....
....
....
....
....
....
....

Saturday ....
....
....
....
....
....
....

Week 23

When another person walks the labyrinth in front of me, and they move slower than I would alone, I'd rather slow down than pass them. It's always fascinating, then, to move more deliberately, each step its own, complete movement, each reverse turn reduced to a slow series of quarter turns. I fall more and more behind, until I forget that person in front of me is even there.

This week: Let something outside of you get you to pay more attention to your own experience.

Sunday

Monday

Tuesday

Wednesday _____

_____

_____

_____

_____

_____

_____

Thursday _____

_____

_____

_____

_____

_____

_____

Friday _____

_____

_____

_____

_____

_____

_____

Saturday _____

_____

_____

_____

_____

_____

_____

Week 24

I sit down on the ground in the center of the labyrinth, having diligently carried my question at the front of my mind through all its loops and reversals. I'm ready now. I'd like my answer now. I plant myself here, waiting, while others come and go, waiting as the sun creeps visibly across the sky. Where is my answer? Hey! I'm here, waiting! Finally, I get up and trudge all the way back to the exit, without my answer.

This week: How do you invite inspiration and guidance? What do you need to do or be, or not do or not be? This week do that, or don't do that, more.

Sunday

Monday

Tuesday

Wednesday _____

_____

_____

_____

_____

_____

_____

Thursday _____

_____

_____

_____

_____

_____

_____

Friday _____

_____

_____

_____

_____

_____

_____

Saturday _____

_____

_____

_____

_____

_____

_____

_____

Week 25

I brought some pebbles in my pocket today while I walk the labyrinth, leaving one perched on a pathway marker stone each time I smile. I brought ten of them, and already ran out.

This week: How many times do you smile in a day? Keep track. Smiling already? That's one.

Sunday ....
....
....
....
....
....
....

Monday ....
....
....
....
....
....

Tuesday ....
....
....
....
....
....
....

Wednesday _____

_____

_____

_____

_____

_____

_____

Thursday _____

_____

_____

_____

_____

_____

_____

Friday _____

_____

_____

_____

_____

_____

_____

Saturday _____

_____

_____

_____

_____

_____

_____

Week 26

Here I am, so close to the center of the labyrinth. I could just step over this one line and already be there. After all, it's only a row of stones some stranger has arranged here. Cheat just a little? Why not?
But wait. Wasn't it me who chose to walk this labyrinth? I wanted this chance for contemplation, opening, connecting, and deepening. Yes, I do want to do this journey. I want to stay on the path.

This week: Are you short-changing yourself in anyway? Are you taking a shortcut that defeats your own best interests? Or are you staying with your chosen path?

Sunday ....
....
....
....
....
....

Monday ....
....
....
....
....
....

Tuesday ....
....
....
....
....
....

Wednesday

Thursday

Friday

Saturday

Week 27

I was going to ask for an answer to a question, but now that I'm standing at the entrance to this labyrinth I'm really not sure that's even the right question to be asking. So, I'm going to ask instead to know what is the right question.

This week: Is there something you're tangled in figuring out? Try a whole different approach this week. See what happens, and journal about it.

Sunday ....
....
....
....
....
....
....

Monday ....
....
....
....
....
....
....

Tuesday ....
....
....
....
....
....
....

Wednesday ....

....

....

....

....

....

....

Thursday ....

....

....

....

....

....

....

Friday ....

....

....

....

....

....

Saturday ....

....

....

....

....

....

....

Week 28

I like outdoor labyrinths. Fresh air, a slight breeze, birds singing, the muted sunlight early or late in the day, blue sky or gray. I like to be alone in a labyrinth. I like to find my own rhythm and take my time. I like to stop and write, not only in the center and afterward, but at any point along the way. I like plants in and around a labyrinth, herbs and flowers, adding their life-filled green and colorful delights. I like firm footing. I like smoothly rounded river stones, and stacks of them at the turns. I like a bench nearby.

This week: Write about your perfect labyrinth. Go online and see if you can find it.

Sunday _____

_____

_____

_____

_____

_____

_____

Monday _____

_____

_____

_____

_____

_____

_____

Tuesday _____

_____

_____

_____

_____

_____

_____

Wednesday

Thursday

Friday

Saturday

Week 29

When walking a labyrinth is a rare opportunity, it's tempting to spend time at the entrance searching for the perfect question or intention. But when easy access allows frequent walking and relaxed familiarity, our whole approach can loosen up. It's a chance to be adventurous, even playful, to experiment, push boundaries, and explore.

This week: What do you do often that you could try playing around with a bit this week? Get creative, try a fun variation, challenge yourself, take a chance.

Sunday ....
....
....
....
....
....
....

Monday ....
....
....
....
....
....
....

Tuesday ....
....
....
....
....
....
....

Wednesday ....
....
....
....
....
....
....

Thursday ....
....
....
....
....
....
....

Friday ....
....
....
....
....
....

Saturday ....
....
....
....
....
....
....

Week 30

Another turn? Already? I stop in the turn of the labyrinth's path and look up at the sky, taking a break from watching my feet. A flotilla of clouds parades overhead, heavy gray, full of moisture, their edges brilliant flares of crystallized sunlight. Beautiful!

This week: When you run into an unexpected turning in your day, look around to see what there is for you to notice.

Sunday ....
....
....
....
....
....
....

Monday ....
....
....
....
....
....
....

Tuesday ....
....
....
....
....
....
....

Wednesday

Thursday

Friday

Saturday

Week 31

I walk to the labyrinth, pause at the entrance, and breathe.
Nothing else matters for the next hour. Everything else drops
away. This is my time to just breathe and walk, and see what
happens. I step in, and follow the path.

This week: Practice this pause. Stop, breathe, let go of every
concern, and simply be in what you are about to do.

Sunday ....

....

....

....

....

....

....

Monday ....

....

....

....

....

....

....

Tuesday ....

....

....

....

....

....

....

Wednesday _____

_____

_____

_____

_____

_____

_____

Thursday _____

_____

_____

_____

_____

_____

_____

Friday _____

_____

_____

_____

_____

_____

_____

Saturday _____

_____

_____

_____

_____

_____

_____

Week 32

The many designs of labyrinths are expressions of sacred patterns behind and beyond all that surrounds us in this physical world. Like the spinning spiral arrangement of a sunflower's seeds, or the whorl of a seashell's architecture, or the pristine facets of crystallized minerals. No wonder we feel we've entered a sacred space. No wonder we are able to go deep into who we really are. No wonder we feel so good inside a labyrinth.

This week: Find some sacred space this week. It's not hard; it's all around us. Write about it.

Sunday

Monday

Tuesday

Wednesday _____

_____

_____

_____

_____

_____

_____

Thursday _____

_____

_____

_____

_____

_____

_____

Friday _____

_____

_____

_____

_____

_____

_____

Saturday _____

_____

_____

_____

_____

_____

_____

Week 33

It's always good when I sit down in the center of the labyrinth and allow time for answers or understanding to come clear. If I hadn't stopped there my mind would have gotten busy with following the path back out and not allowed anything juicy to rise up.

This week: Notice when you keep moving and when you slow down to allow knowing.

Sunday ....
....
....
....
....
....
....

Monday ....
....
....
....
....
....
....

Tuesday ....
....
....
....
....
....
....

Wednesday _____
_____
_____
_____
_____
_____
_____

Thursday _____
_____
_____
_____
_____
_____

Friday _____
_____
_____
_____
_____
_____

Saturday _____
_____
_____
_____
_____
_____
_____

Week 34

A friend had back surgery and recovery took five weeks. I brought her one of Laurel Reinhardt's quilted lap labyrinths (www.etsy.com/shop/InnerLandscaping), for finger walking. She traced its path to "walk" it every day. Visitors who had never walked a labyrinth saw it and "walked" it, too.

This week: Remember your first labyrinth walk? How is labyrinth walking different or the same now?

Sunday
....
....
....
....
....
....
....

Monday
....
....
....
....
....
....
....

Tuesday
....
....
....
....
....
....

Wednesday _____

_____

_____

_____

_____

_____

_____

Thursday _____

_____

_____

_____

_____

_____

Friday _____

_____

_____

_____

_____

_____

Saturday _____

_____

_____

_____

_____

_____

_____

Week 35

This time the answer to my question came at the fourth turn of the labyrinth's path, instead of waiting for my arrival at the center. There it was, just as I turned the corner. If I'd been hurrying to get to the center, I might have blown on past and missed it. Good thing I was willing to notice when it came early.

This week: Answers, solutions, discoveries, and new connections can appear at any time. Are you available to notice them? This week explore how you can catch more of these off-center revelations.

Sunday ....
....
....
....
....
....
....

Monday ....
....
....
....
....
....
....

Tuesday ....
....
....
....
....
....
....

Wednesday --

Thursday ---

Friday ---

Saturday --

Week 36

Sometimes those long outer labyrinth runs go on and on and on, tedious, endless, and disappointingly, frustratingly far from focused center. And I think, will I ever get on with this? Or...aha! This is all about learning patience, perseverance, commitment, and trust. I take a deep breath, settle in, walk the walk, and it works. I arrive at the center.

This week: What in your life seems stuck in a rut, forever recycling the familiar? Is there more going on than is apparent?

Sunday

Monday

Tuesday

Wednesday ....
....
....
....
....
....
....

Thursday ....
....
....
....
....
....
....

Friday ....
....
....
....
....
....

Saturday ....
....
....
....
....
....
....

Week 37

This is the first labyrinth I ever walked, many years ago, when I'd just begun to consider ending my marriage. I've brought a stone from my new life to leave in this labyrinth to mark and connect and heal the fragments of my path.

This week: Is there something you would like to release or memorialize or set to rest? Find an earthy, simple stone, add it to the others of a labyrinth, and let it go.

Sunday ....
....
....
....
....
....
....

Monday ....
....
....
....
....
....
....

Tuesday ....
....
....
....
....
....
....

Wednesday

Thursday

Friday

Saturday

Week 38

Back again at the opening, about to step out of the labyrinth, I survey the everyday world ahead. Walking a labyrinth changes me. Priorities rearrange, concerns drop away. Breath now matters, heart matters, connection matters, meaning matters. Everything now is ripe, potent, and possible. Full of grace.

This week: Each day close your eyes and go back into that feeling of having walked a labyrinth. See how that changes your perspective on this day.

Sunday ....
....
....
....
....
....
....

Monday ....
....
....
....
....
....
....

Tuesday ....
....
....
....
....
....
....

Wednesday ....
....
....
....
....
....
....

Thursday ....
....
....
....
....
....
....

Friday ....
....
....
....
....
....

Saturday ....
....
....
....
....
....
....

Week 39

I stand at the entrance to the labyrinth, looking for a meaningful question or intention to carry with me into its deepening, in hopes of clarity, new knowing, or a cleansing release.

This week: What do you want to improve or understand or resolve as you head into this next day?

Sunday ....
....
....
....
....
....
....

Monday ....
....
....
....
....
....
....

Tuesday ....
....
....
....
....
....
....

Wednesday --

Thursday ---

Friday ---

Saturday ---

Week 40

I used to get frustrated when turns in a labyrinth broke into my rhythm, forced me to backtrack, headed me off in the wrong direction, and foiled my efforts to get anywhere. Then I got it. A labyrinth is a microcosm of life, and life never goes in straight lines. Complications and distractions in our days constantly force us to divert our attention and change directions. Now I see a labyrinth's complexity as a chance to practice patience and to trust that the journey works.

This week: Watch for your chance to practice patience and trust. Write about it.

Sunday

Monday

Tuesday

Wednesday

Thursday

Friday

Saturday

Week 41

A labyrinth challenges us to be more than we already are, to express more of our possibilities, to expand into more of all we can be. When a labyrinth draws our attention, and then draws us inside to walk it, we open the door to explore what else there is to life and what else there is in us.

This week: What more might you be, or do, or create, or offer, or make happen? This week figure out the first step and do it.

Sunday ....
....
....
....
....
....
....

Monday ....
....
....
....
....
....
....

Tuesday ....
....
....
....
....
....
....

Wednesday _____
_____
_____
_____
_____
_____
_____

Thursday _____
_____
_____
_____
_____
_____
_____

Friday _____
_____
_____
_____
_____
_____

Saturday _____
_____
_____
_____
_____
_____
_____

Week 42

Ouch! Stubbed my toe! The narrow, uneven paths of this labyrinth are lined with big stones, and one got me. Okay, I did take my eyes off the path for a couple of seconds to check my phone. But hey! Who put that oversized lump of a rock right there next to the turn, anyway?

This week: I'm going to take more responsibility for what happens to me. Will you join me? Write about how you do better at that each day.

Sunday ....

....

....

....

....

....

Monday ....

....

....

....

....

....

Tuesday ....

....

....

....

....

....

Wednesday _____

_____

_____

_____

_____

_____

_____

Thursday _____

_____

_____

_____

_____

_____

_____

Friday _____

_____

_____

_____

_____

_____

Saturday _____

_____

_____

_____

_____

_____

_____

Week 43

I sit on the bench at the edge of the labyrinth with four big questions swirling in my head, wanting to bring all of them into the labyrinth today, all necessary and urgent, needing answers. It's too much, I know.

After some deep, slow breaths the solution comes to me. Ask, instead, to learn where to place a single, primary focus, and let the rest of this complexity go. Yes. What a relief!

This week: Is there too much complexity in some area of your life? Look for how you can simplify and focus today.

Sunday

Monday

Tuesday

Wednesday --

Thursday --

Friday --

Saturday --

Week 44

Labyrinths are being constructed with all sorts of materials these days: laid out with field stones, bricks, wine bottles, earthworks, herbs and flowering plants, candles, wood, gravel, paint, bamboo, crushed limestone, cobblestones, concrete, turf, sand, tiles, and more.

This week: Think of something you do every day. Do it a new way today, and write about it.

Sunday ....
....
....
....
....
....
....

Monday ....
....
....
....
....
....
....

Tuesday ....
....
....
....
....
....
....

Wednesday

Thursday

Friday

Saturday

Week 45

I've barely started to walk this labyrinth when I find myself suddenly, astonishingly quite near the center. How exciting! Already here! Without all that journeying, none of those endless steps and turnings and time to deepen. It's so easy. Except... What's this? Turning away? Back out? Back to twists and turns and walking the walk? Back out into life's journeying?

This week: What stays at arm's length in your life, still not quite reachable? What can you do about that today?

Sunday

Monday

Tuesday

Wednesday

Thursday

Friday

Saturday

Week 46

Have you walked one of the big cathedral labyrinths? With the high, vaulted ceiling and clusters of tall, vertical columns. Stained glass windows admitting impossibly ethereal light. The air flavored by a many-layered mixture of incense, wax candles, and wood polish. Faces of saints, as statue and spirit, watch, holding the space for your journey. Footsteps echo up and down the nave. You walk, barely breathing, carefully placing one foot, then the other, sensing sacred ground.

This week: If you can walk a labyrinth inside a church this week, go. Or, one in the woods or on a hilltop will do as well.

Sunday

Monday

Tuesday

Wednesday

Thursday

Friday

Saturday

Week 47

I went into the labyrinth with a full load of grief,
   and came out comforted.
I went into the labyrinth with questions,
   and came out with a sense of direction.
I went into the labyrinth discouraged,
   and came out full of grace.
I went into the labyrinth angry, and came out forgiven.
I went into the labyrinth grateful, and came out blessed.

This week: What would you like to happen when you walk a labyrinth today?

Sunday

Monday

Tuesday

Wednesday --

Thursday --

Friday --

Saturday --

Week 48

There was another place to be and no time, so I cut across the labyrinth's paths to get to the exit fast. It felt wrong before I even got there, and worse later. Like waking up suddenly in the middle of the night, no gentle re-entry, no getting my bearings. It left me disoriented, ungrounded, and really not safe to drive the car.

This week: Watch for any short cuts you take. Does it put you where you want to be, or does it throw you off kilter?

Sunday

Monday

Tuesday

Wednesday _____

_____

_____

_____

_____

_____

_____

Thursday _____

_____

_____

_____

_____

_____

_____

Friday _____

_____

_____

_____

_____

_____

Saturday _____

_____

_____

_____

_____

_____

_____

Week 49

I came to the labyrinth today with an important question, looking for guidance. But I became so engrossed in walking its winding paths that when I got to the center the question was gone from my mind. Maybe it wasn't so important after all.

This week: Stop each day and ask yourself if what seems so important today really is.

Sunday _____
_____
_____
_____
_____
_____
_____

Monday _____
_____
_____
_____
_____
_____
_____

Tuesday _____
_____
_____
_____
_____
_____
_____

Wednesday ....
....
....
....
....
....
....

Thursday ....
....
....
....
....
....
....

Friday ....
....
....
....
....
....
....

Saturday ....
....
....
....
....
....
....

Week 50

As I walk back out from the center of the labyrinth, reversing the steps that 20-minutes before took me into deep contemplation, I bring with me a renewed sense of meaning, intention, and spiritual awareness. With each step I feel more solid, and more prepared to re-enter daily life. I'm very aware of being both physical and mystical. I feel very alive.

This week: How can you awaken your own sense of aliveness today? Do it, and journal about it.

Sunday ....

....

....

....

....

....

....

Monday ....

....

....

....

....

....

....

Tuesday ....

....

....

....

....

....

....

Wednesday _____
_____
_____
_____
_____
_____
_____

Thursday _____
_____
_____
_____
_____
_____
_____

Friday _____
_____
_____
_____
_____
_____
_____

Saturday _____
_____
_____
_____
_____
_____
_____

Week 51

Walking a candlelit outdoor labyrinth on a gentle spring evening as dusk settles is one of the most beautiful experiences of life. Or, there is a dawn labyrinth walk, as the birds build their joyful morning chorus. Or walk during a midday summer rain with bare feet and an umbrella. Or beneath the shadowy new moon at midnight with a small flashlight focused at your feet, abandoning bearings and simply being in each few footsteps.

This week: Look for ways to make each of your days special, even magical or extraordinary. Write about what works.

Sunday

Monday

Tuesday

Wednesday

Thursday

Friday

Saturday

Week 52

A labyrinth always returns me to where I entered. I may be changed, I may have a new perspective or a new intention, but I recognize and know where I am. It delivers me to emerge into a fresh start.

This week: Find a way to make a fresh start in some area of your life today. Journal about it.

Sunday ....
....
....
....
....
....
....

Monday ....
....
....
....
....
....
....

Tuesday ....
....
....
....
....
....
....

Wednesday

Thursday

Friday

Saturday

Dear friend,

I hope you enjoyed your year of journaling in the labyrinth. Please don't stop now. Keep writing about your own labyrinth experiences, and how they relate to the rest of your life.

Namaste,
Aliyah Schick

Books by Aliyah Schick

- Angels Meditative Coloring Book 1
- Crosses Meditative Coloring Book 2
- Ancient Symbols Meditative Coloring Book 3
- Hearts Meditative Coloring Book 4
- Labyrinths Meditative Coloring Book 5
- OM Meditative Coloring Book 6

- The Labyrinth Guided Journal

- Chai Jewish Coloring Book for Grown Ups
- Star of David Jewish Coloring Book for Grown Ups
- Alefbet Jewish Coloring Book for Grown Ups
- Judaica Jewish Coloring Book for Grown Ups

- Mary Magdalene's Words: Two Women's Spiritual Journey, Both Truth and Fiction, Both Ancient and Now.
- The Mary Magdalene Book: Mary Magdalene Speaks, Her Story and Her Message
- Finally, a Book of Poetry by Aliyah Schick

For new and future Guided Journals, or for the Meditative Coloring Books, and other books by author/artist Aliyah Schick visit:

www.amazon.com/author/AliyahSchick

www.SacredImprints.com

CPSIA information can be obtained at www.ICGtesting.com
Printed in the USA
LVOW08s2145270616

494268LV00001BA/212/P